Fragments

Freya Petterson

BookLeaf Publishing

Fragments © 2022

Freya Petterson

All rights reserved.

No part of this publication may be
reproduced, stored in a retrieval system, or
transmitted, in any form or by any means,
electronic, mechanical, photocopying,
recording or otherwise, without the prior
written permission of the presenters.

Freya Petterson asserts the moral right to be
identified as the author of this work.

Presentation by *BookLeaf Publishing*

Web: www.bookleafpub.com

E-mail: info@bookleafpub.com

ISBN: 9789357612067

First edition 2022

Dedicated to my dearest mama, if I am your sunshine then it is only because you have been my world. Thank you for everything.

I think I need to lay down, mum

My vision periscopes
And everything in view becomes
A mishmash of blended colours
A craft hour press-together-pull-apart butterfly
painting
Life through a kaleidoscope

My Body

The body is a resilient thing
The lengths it will go to, to keep me alive
The body will cut off its own limb to save the
whole.
The body will cut off its own head to save the
whole.

My body will carve out memories – a
melon-baller to a honeydew
It's to protect me,
Of course.

My body will switch off the lights – so nobody
can find me
I can no longer find me

My body - It's my body.
I didn't choose to do this to my body.

Did you mean: am I dying?

Your body is your doctor.
They flirt with you / They dare you to guess
what is wrong

You have a list of symptoms and your mum's
medical textbook
Fifty minutes now and then pencils down.

Your body, I say, but isn't it my body?
Your body My body
It sends you on a scavenger hunt.

On hands and knees, shoving 'growing pains'
and 'constant fear' together
Maybe Google will pat you on the back and put
you to bed – tell you goodnight
You might be dying?

The ache in my ribs is a puzzle piece – fragile,
waterlogged, and illegible.

I ask my body "what is wrong with you?"
The first hint is sharp, metal on my tongue
Twelve letters, three up and four across

I haven't kept food down in days

It is begging now
"What is wrong with you?"

My body, arrogant and gloating – she thinks
she's got a fucking medical degree.
Waits for me to finish this dot-to-dot
Promises me I'll start to see the big picture

It takes a week
A week before I understand, and cry for how
awfully hungry I'd been
I eat yogurt at gunpoint

I had a migraine for five hours before my body
told me about it.
Drink water. Rest. Drink more water. Eat.
But I had a migraine? I should have just taken a
painkiller and been done with it. Christ.

Who gave you the right?

Painful Clarity

If I close my eyes / I am in bed
The curtains are drawn, and the rain patters far
overhead
Someone in a nearby apartment
Plays piano
A song I don't recognise,

I open my eyes / I am standing
Under the neon umbrella of a fish and chip
storefront
It is pouring down torrential rain
The air is much too cold
Sound is too harsh to my ears,

I close my eyes,
Just to blink / and in that split second

I am home again
It feels like vertigo
Like motion sickness

Again now / I am on a train
Sitting in the last carriage in the furthest seat
The whistling is white noise
Until I close my eyes
And there is no whistling in my bedroom,

When I am home / I have been home
It is a violent déjà vu to enter here
Peeling off bags and clothing
Like soiled bandages

To pull drawn my curtains and hide
My body under a heavy duvet

Reality meshes with a dizzying clarity
This dichotomy can now be lain down to rest
I am left   shaky,   jittery,   nauseous.

Epi-Pen

When I was old enough to talk, someone handed
me an epi-pen.
"You don't know this yet. But sometimes
innocuous events will become large and scary,
and they will try to hurt you."
I wasn't told how to tell the difference.
I'm not allergic to shellfish or peanuts. I'm not
allergic to anything. Maybe it's a moment of
not-so-subtle irony?
I might be allergic to loud noises / Sometimes I
am not.
Or maybe movies / Sometimes I am not.
It must be one of the ingredients? Right?
But life happens on a tilt slide and you can't
pause the screen to pull up a list of [main
allergies present]
You can only ever guess.
I don't have an epi-pen. I don't know why I
thought I did?

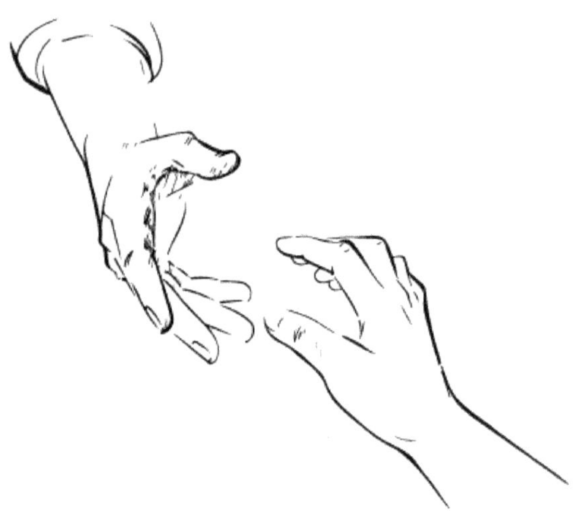

Places

I believe that when you call a place a home and
live within it
You leave pieces of yourself behind when
you've gone
I feel it sometimes in old churches, and hospitals
– the home of a loving and loved family three
generations forward.
I have lived here for so short a time, but I will
leave it so heavy with grief.
I have walked within buildings and felt their
second-hand pain, centuries old sorrow reflected
outwards,
And I have known doubtlessly that someone has
hurt whilst living here, in these walls – will my
walls become this to another?
What is a place but a memorial?
Ghosts are not always shades of death, but more
often they are memories that became stuck to a
place. A long-kept journal swollen with words,
no real added mass and yet so irrevocably
changed – larger by its sorrows.
Every action has a consequence, you cannot
exist without touching something.
I wonder, can I take back my grief? Is it still
mine to take, or just another ghost of a girl who

looks a lot like me, who once lived here, who still lives here, who will always live here?

Exceptions to the Rule

I am cold, tired, and lonely.
But I will stay with you
If I stay, maybe I will find a way to help you?

If I stay, and if staying here hurts me
Is it worth the relief I could herald in?
Just how far can this justification take me?

If I allow myself to stay, allow myself to suffer
Is it worth it?
Am I doing the right thing?

What are these boundaries we build up like
moral tent pegs stuck in wet sand?
Self-serving idealism leaves no room for error
The drowning man pulls everyone down with
him
Would it be better to protect myself?
Is it correct to do so?

Morality is not stagnant
Your limits will be superseded,
You must break and change.
Circumstance will require you to go beyond
yourself to save those you love.

How many times?

What if my inaction hurts you?
Could I live with that - live with myself?
Isn't it safer to be hurt?

If the exception is not the rule, then when do I
make an exception?
What will happen if I make a mistake?
Is putting myself first supposed to hurt so bad?

Does self-preservation still matter in the face of
your suffering?

Self Love

Braiding my hair like a mother might
Hurried French plaits for picture day
Swift deliberate fingers on soft child's hair

I weep for the girl with my face
With a life that may have been mine
And a heart so much easier to love

For a moment I entertain unequivocal
Unconditional forgiveness and
It hurts me

To life my face up the sky as it breaks
Open above, finally making peace with
This loneliness
Learn to give her a name

Maybe I could learn to live like this?
Can anyone live like this?

Is everyone living like this?

How Dare You, I Will Not Forgive

Forgiveness is a burden
The child is screaming "look! I am angry! I am
hurting!"
This is how we grow

I watch tantrums with a quiet and shameful envy
I want to cry and scream alongside her - I want
to be angry

Instead I have to be "I understand. You didn't
mean to hurt me. I will
forgive you"

Holding back, waiting to see if I am loved
enough
To merit an apology
Feels like something sinfully hedonistic
My vice is my anger, and I will abstain abstain
abstain

There can be power in forgiveness
In "I understand why you hurt me the way you
did"
There can also be power in steadfastness

In "I will never understand, my anger is
justified, and I refuse to falter"

I mean honestly? We all know how to say sorry
They taught us before we could speak
I do not know how to be angry
And still be a person

Am I allowed this? Am I owed this?
Is it not easier to exercise compassion?
To just forgive?
Easier for whom?
Not me.

Suffering ≠ Salvation

Guilt is not a virtue, nor suffering a judgement
of character
Your hardships are not permission slips –
'If I suffer enough, then I can justify my hurting'

No one survives solitude. Death by lonesome.

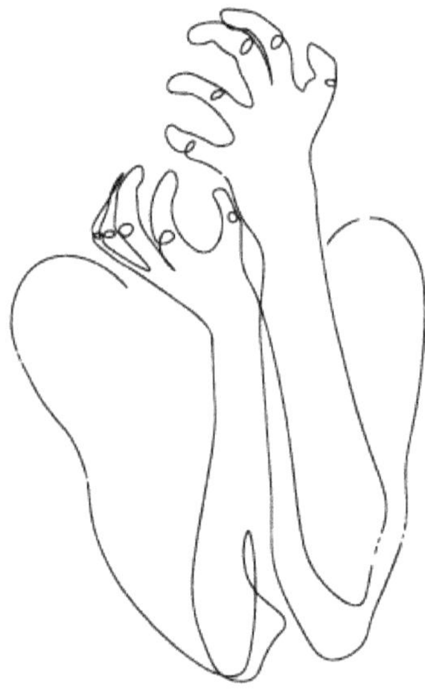

"It is all Grey"

"You don't understand. This is just a grey area,
right and wrong cannot exist here."

Okay, so show me where. Show me this grey.
Take my hand, let us take out a map
And you point me towards what is grey.

It's all grey though, isn't it?

You like to believe in evil and good
It's so easy to fall back upon
Justified and condemned.
It is so rarely ever this simple.
We think that we understand this.

An evil act will come to a head
But its body will be human
-          Your neighbour, your brother, yourself?

It is so incredibly messy to navigate
But this lego strewn on the floor is dangerous
You have grown much too old,
Your mother won't clear it up for you now

You must confront it.
Face this greyscale and ask it its name.

Angels on Earth

Angels on Earth struggling to find meaning:
The struggle between righteous fury and
shameful kindness.

Is humanity the goal or the consequence?

Forever is an awfully long time for an absence
of meaning. Where there is love, there is
meaning. Where there is mud, there is water.
Where there is hatred, there is meaning on a tilt
scale, head upturned and limbs flailing.
I am angry, so so angry.
But creation from anger is so typical and boring.
I want to be drowning in love and create
miracles through my enduring grace.
Angels on Earth trying to find peace, but never
knowing how to hold it.
Love in a closed fist, love in a loose thread, love
caught between your teeth.
Peace does not feel real, like pain does. It is not
loud and belligerent.
Peace is quiet and comfortable, it will never cry
like pain does.

Someone Who is Not Me

Sometimes in late moments - in quiet and
Terrified moments –
I will pretend that somebody is holding my
hand.

It gets tiring being strong.

My wellbeing is not your responsibility,
It isn't on you, as much as you love me
And I love you

(I wish it was somebody's responsibility though
– Someone else who isn't me.)

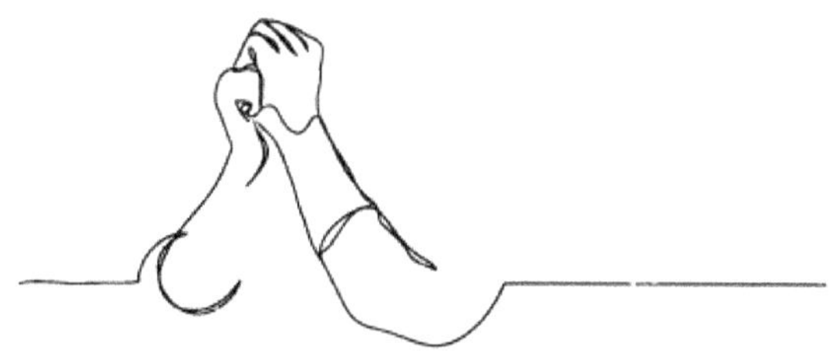

Tank the Market Value

You say to me: "I am giving you my love"
Well then how will you give it to me?
How shall I prepare myself to receive it?
Love is a verb, not simply a noun.
Loving comes easy, I draw from a bottomless
well
I take in handfuls and big shuddering gulps
Fill up my cheeks to the bursting

* * *

Hey hey, babe, did you know that I'm
Well, I'm just full of love?
Just steeped overnight in it, brimming with it
So utterly consumed with thoughts of love
Love, love love!
It resonates within me
A chord strung long and somewhere deep
Echoing around this great big hall
Now all this love is just gushing up, crashing
waves
Feels like I could snort it out my nose like a
milkshake
Tap it out my ears like pool water
Babe, I feel effervescent
I feel charged

In this brief beautiful morning I could fill up the
whole world
And make love a plentiful resource
Tank it's market value, create a hyperinflation
Steal the monopoly that exists to hoard love
away
I could keep us all in love and we would never
go hungry

Warm

The water is still lukewarm
The thermostat is maxed
And my skin is an angry red

I really wanted to be warm
All I've ever wanted was to be warm

And why settle?
If I am already red, raw, and burning
Why be cautious?
I think I would rather be warm

Burning

If it's going to blister
It may as well burn
And if it's going to Burn
Then it may as well Blaze.
If it's going to graze it may as well cut
And if it's going to cut
It may as well Cleave.

I sit in a crowded hall and play with my hands
on my lap
Seconds pass in minutes, hours in fragments
And then it is over
And I am Bleeding

If it cuts it may as well Bleed
And if it bleeds then it might as well Hurt
I prefer it hurting.

If it is going to hurt then I want it to hurt me
loud
I want it to try to kill me
And I don't want the assurance of knowing it
won't
I prefer it hurting.
The alternative is too bleak to ponder.

Where is all this light coming from?

you have yourself
and only
yourself
(to blame?)
to love

Securities

I used to be secure in what I knew
I could always go home
I could always call my mum
and she would always come to pick me up

In every moment where I was scared
and when I was alone
that safety was a blanket I could always
reach for

I don't have that anymore
I saw my home become barren and useless
and my mum asked me once if I knew how to
save
her, and she told me that she was
relying on me now.
So what can I do?

How do I go home when home is only a memory

I feel scared and suddenly I am five years
old on my first day of school and I'm
standing alone
and I want to call my mum. I want to call my
mum. I want my mum.
but I can still see her grown small and distant

hear her calling for me
and I can't make that phone call anymore

I will still love you after this is all over

The thing that is but is not now what it was
A declarative admission
I am changed, I am anew
I cannot be hurt again by you

The place that was then is now no longer
Can you live with yourself?
How can you live with yourself?

I have watched louder, braver girls
And I have felt very small
I have to live with myself too, you know

Come to me grovelling and repentant
And then, only then, will I forgive you
And I will love you all the same

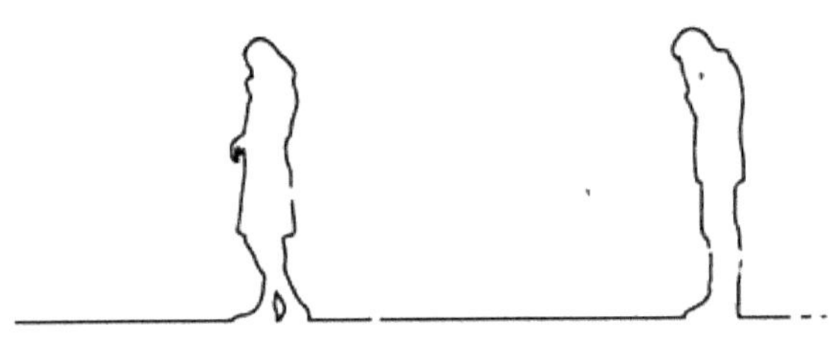